DOODLE THROUGH GOD'S CREATION FOR KIDS

JONNY HAWKINS

HARVEST kids™

HARVEST HOUSE PUBLISHERS
EUGENE, OREGON

Unless otherwise indicated, Scripture paraphrases are by the author.

Scripture quotations marked NLT are taken from the *Holy Bible*, New Living Translation, copyright ©1996, 2004, 2007, 2013 by Tyndale House Foundation. Used by permission of Tyndale House Publishers, Inc., Carol Stream, Illinois 60188. All rights reserved.

Cover design by Dugan Design Group

HARVEST KIDS is a registered trademark of The Hawkins Children's LLC. Harvest House Publishers, Inc., is the exclusive licensee of the federally registered trademark HARVEST KIDS.

DOODLE THROUGH GOD'S CREATION FOR KIDS

Copyright © 2018 by Jonny Hawkins
Published by Harvest House Publishers
Eugene, Oregon 97408
www.harvesthousepublishers.com

ISBN 978-0-7369-7194-2 (pbk.)

Printed in the United States of America

17 18 19 20 21 22 23 24 /VP-CD/ 10 9 8 7 6 5 4 3 2 1

COLOR ME!

DOODLE OTHER RED ITEMS GOD HAS MADE

DOODLE ORANGE CREATED THINGS.

(A fleet of navels?)

YELLOW...

GREEN...

(SO APPEELING!)

BLUE...

INDIGO AND VIOLET...

(DON'T BE BLUE!)

(NOT YOUR HAIR!)

LIST FIVE FAVORITE OTHER COLORS GOD HAS MADE!

1. _____ 2. _____
3. _____ 4. _____
5. _____

THIS SAYS "PRAISE GOD" IN DIFFERENT LANGUAGES. PICK ONE AND WRITE IT IN BUBBLE LETTERS IN THE CURVED BOX.

alabado sea el Señor
SPANISH

Louange à Dieu
FRENCH

слава Богу
RUSSIAN

lodare Dio
ITALIAN

Chwalić Boga
POLISH

Lob Gott
GERMAN

LANGUAGES CAME ABOUT AT THE TOWER OF BABEL WHEN GOD CONFUSED THE PEOPLE WHO WERE BUILDING A TOWER TO THE HEAVENS TO MAKE A NAME FOR THEM- SELVES. THEY WERE SCATTERED ALL OVER THE EARTH LIKE SAND.

Praying Mantis

WHERE IS SHE PRAYING? DOODLE IT!

GOD USES EVEN CRITTERS TO REMIND US OF HIM.
HOW DID HE USE LOCUSTS IN THE OLD TESTAMENT
TO FREE THE ISRAELITES? IF IT DOESN'T BUG YOU, DOODLE A SWARM.

DOODLE JURY MEMBERS

DOODLE A FAIR (JUST) BUT LOVING JUDGE. (DON'T FORGET THE HAMMER!)

JESUS RE-STATED THE IMPORTANCE OF THE TEN COMMANDMENTS IN MATTHEW 22:36-39, WHICH HE SHORTENED TO THESE TWO:

1) _____   2) _____

GLADNESS

SURPRISE

Fill IN THE BLANK FACES

SADNESS

SO SERIOUS

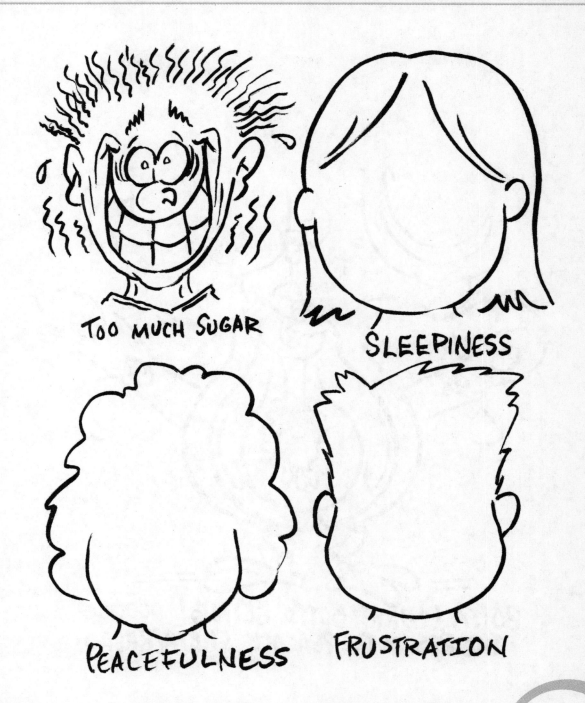

TOO MUCH SUGAR

SLEEPINESS

PEACEFULNESS

FRUSTRATION

BOTTA PLUME, BOTTA BLING! DOODLE THE REST OF THE PEACOCK, FEATHERHEAD!

IN THIS PASSAGE, ELIJAH IS TAKEN UP TO HEAVEN BY WHIRLWIND IN A CHARIOT OF FIRE!... ...AND HORSES OF FIRE! FINISH THIS FIERY HORSEPOWER!

VICTORIA FALLS IN AFRICA IS THE LARGEST WATERFALL IN THE WORLD. IT WAS DISCOVERED BY EXPLORER AND MISSIONARY DAVID LIVINGSTONE.

DOODLE OTHER AFRICAN WILDLIFE THAT ARE
TAKING THE WILD RIDE OVER THE FALLS ...WITH
THEIR BACKPACK PARACHUTES ON, OF COURSE.
FINISH THE LOG RAFTS AS WELL.

ANY OTHER BARNSTORMING MUSICIANS? DOODLE THEM.

GOD HAS PLACED ALL KINDS OF MUSIC
IN OUR HEADS AND HEARTS FOR US TO ENJOY.
THIS COW MAKES GREAT MOO-SIC.

SOLVE THE PICTURE PUZZLES TO IDENTIFY THE STYLE OF MUSIC (NAME THAT 'TOON!). THEN, DOODLE THE STYLE WRITTEN IN THE WORD BOXES. ANSWERS AT BOTTOM

1) ROCK AND ROLL 2) BLUE GRASS 3) HIP HOP 4) ELEVATOR 5) OPERA

Musical Instruments

TAKE NOTE AND PICK UP YOUR PIG PEN AND SEE IF YOU CAN MAKE IT FROM ONE END OF THE EUPHONIUM TO THE OTHER WITHOUT LIFTING IT. EUPHORIA! (HAPPINESS) GO FROM NOTE TO NOTE.

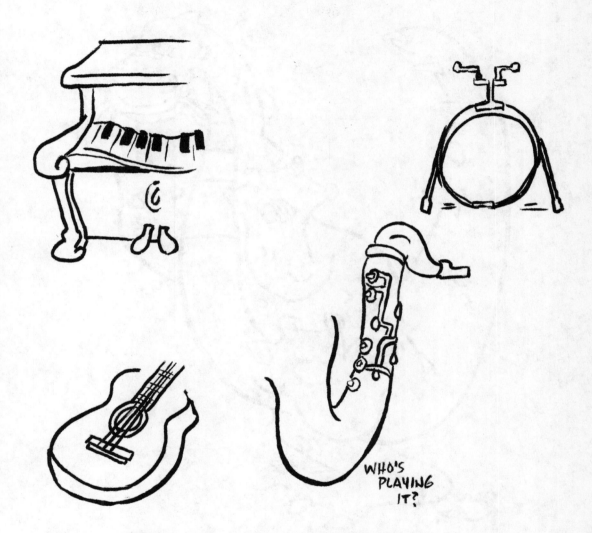

WHO'S
PLAYING
IT?

GOD FASHIONED MAN, WHO MAKES MUSIC AND
INSTRUMENTS, TO PRAISE HIM. FINISH THESE PIECES
AND MAKE AN ANIMAL BRASS PLAYER! A FOX ON SAX?

CAN YOU DOODLE THE MIGHTY CREATURE, THE BEHEMOTH, AS GOD DESCRIBED IT TO JOB IN THIS PASSAGE?

He's GOT MAIL

FINISH THIS MIGHTY AND AMAZING SEA CREATURE! DON'T FORGET HIS 'DOUBLE MAIL' AND OTHER AWESOME FEATURES!

SWIMMING WITH THIS FIRE BREATHER COULD GET YOU IN REAL HOT WATER!

PICK UP YOUR PEN AND FOLLOW THE SNAIL TRAIL STARTING AT "YOU!" DON'T SNOOZE TILL YOU REACH THE WIZARD OF OOZE.

CAN YOU DESIGN AN AMAZING MAZE WITH SLUG SLIME? OOZE IT OR LOSE IT!

Gold and Honey

DOODLE THIS DIGGER STRIKING GOLD!
USE GOLD BARS TO SPELL OUT "FEAR OF THE LORD."

SHOW THE INNER WORKINGS OF A
HONEY COMB. SWEET!

FEAST YOUR EYES ON DELICIOUS DELIGHTS!
TO DOODLE FOOD'LL SHOW HOW GOOD GOD IS!

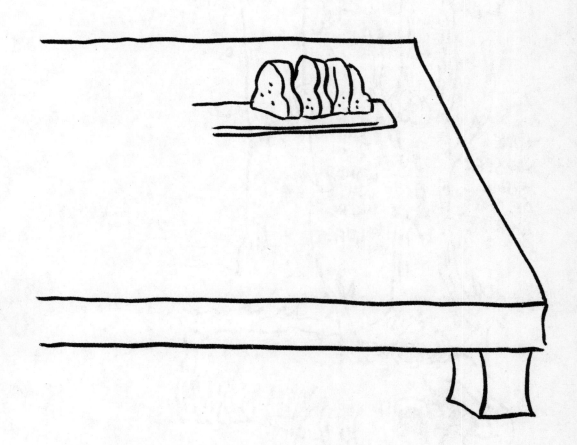

CAN YOU DOODLE A POODLE? OR OTHER DOGS BEGGING FOR A BAGEL? (LIKE A BEAGLE!)

PETRIFIED FOREST NATIONAL PARK IN ARIZONA IS KNOWN FOR ITS REDWOODS, PETRIFIED (ROCK HARD) WOOD AND FOSSILS ON 230 SQUARE MILES. IT IS A SIGHT TO SEE! WOOD YOU FINISH THE FOREST?

WHAT IN THE FOREST FRIGHTENS YOU? ARE YOU AFRAID TO DOODLE IT? WHAT HELPS YOU WITH THE FEAR? PICTURE IT IF YOU CAN.

DOODLE A SPARROW
FINDING A HOME
(IS IT NARROW?)

DOODLE A BETTER HOME
FOR A SWALLOW.
(IS IT HOLLOW?)

HOW MANY DIFFERENT TYPES OF BIRDS
CAN YOU DOODLE? FINCH? PHEASANT? ROBIN?
(IS THAT A FEATHER PEN?)

HUMP DAY! WHO IS LEADING THE CAMEL?
DOODLE THE WILDERNESS BECOMING A
POOL OF WATER.

I'LL SPOT YOU A FISH.

DO YOU HAVE CURLY HAIR, BLUE EYES, BIG FEET, FRECKLES, KINDA ROUND, MUSCLES, KINDA BROWN?

GOD HAS HAND-CRAFTED YOU, AS DAVID SAID, "YOU KNIT ME TOGETHER IN MY MOTHER'S WOMB." WE'VE ALL BEEN KNIT BY HIM, WHICH MEANS WE CAN BE CLOSE-KNIT. HE KNIT MY WIT. SOME SAY I'M A NITWIT!

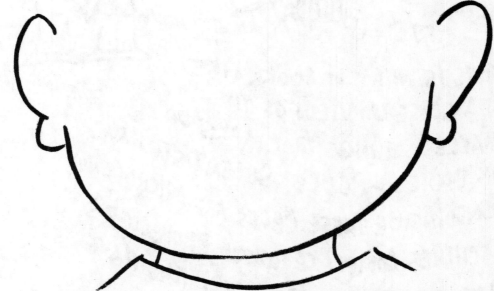

GOD HAS MADE OUR EYES TO BLINK 28,000 TIMES A DAY... TO GIVE OUR BRAINS MICRO-RESTS. NO TIME TO REST NOW, THOUGH! EXPRESS YOURSELF AND DO SOME FACE TIME... AND HAIR! THEN... ZZZZ

THIS IS WHAT IT LOOKS LIKE IN A CLOSE-UP VIEW OF THE SMALLEST THINGS THAT MAKE UP OUR BODIES - CELLS. SCIENTISTS HAVE FOUND INSIDE THESE CELLS ARE MICRO(TINY) MACHINES COMPLETE WITH PROPELLERS THAT RUN OUR BODIES. COULD THIS HAVE HAPPENED OVER TIME BY CHANCE? NOT A CHANCE! GOD IS THE MICRO-MACHINIST - THE CREATOR AND MASTER MECHANIC!

DOODLE WHAT YOU
LOOKED LIKE BEFORE YOU
WERE BORN.

DAVID SAYS, "GOD SAW MY UNFORMED SUBSTANCE
(BODY)." EVEN BEFORE WE WERE IN MOMMY'S
TUMMY, GOD KNEW US!

HAVE SOME ELEFUN AND USE YOUR GRAY MATTER TO DOODLE OTHER GRAY CRITTERS ON THIS BIG BEAST.

DOODLE HOW GOD FEEDS THE CRAVIN' RAVEN ...
AND DRAW A HOT DISH OF SLUG-GHETTI AND MITE BALLS!

CHECK OUT THESE RUG CUTTING DANCERS!

MACARONI DOING THE MACARENA

ENTOMOLOGIST DANCING THE JITTER BUG

FISHERMAN DOING "THE WORM"

TRAIN ENGINEER DOING THE CHA-CHA NEAR HIS CHOO-CHOO!

DOODLE DIFFERENT DANCERS DOING DIFFERENT
DANCES...SWING, TAP, SLIDE!

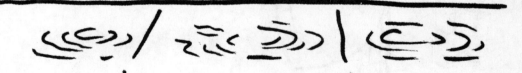

THERE ARE ALL KINDS OF WACKY DANCES —
LIKE THE MOON WALK, RAIN DANCE, POLKA DOT
DANCING — OK, I'M NOT EXACTLY SPOT ON WITH THAT ONE.
GOD HAS MADE US TO MOVE IN MANY AMAZING WAYS.
HE WANTS US MOST OF ALL TO DANCE FOR JOY IN HIM!

DOODLE AN ARMY ANT NEXT TO THIS CARPENTER ANT!

DON'T BE LAZY!
DOODLE A WHOLE COLONY
MARCHING TO THEIR UNDERGROUND CHURCH!

GOD IS SO CREATIVE, HE MADE
TOO MANY VARIETIES TO NAME —
UNLESS YOU'RE A BEAN COUNTER.
HOW MUCH MORE HAS HE PUT INTO US HUMAN BEANS!

Jelly Bean   Peanut

BEANIE BABIES

OVER 40,000 BEANS COVER THE EARTH - LIKE IN
BEANTOWN (BOSTON) AND BEANSYLVANIA! CAN YOU COME UP
WITH SOME FUN CREATED BEANS TO COVER THIS PAGE?

WHO'S SO FINE ON THE VINE?

FASHION A CROWN FOR "THE KING OF THE JUNGLE"

THERE ARE MANY SIZED CATS IN THE FAMILY- FROM THE LION TO THE TIGER TO THE CHEETAH TO..UH...WELL, YOUR HOUSE CAT. WHAT CREA-CATiViTY!

TWO
LIPS

AFTER YOU DOODLE THEM,
ADD SOME FLOWERY COLORS... LET IT GROW!

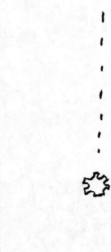

GOD SAYS WHEN WE ASK HIS FORGIVENESS,
HE MAKES OUR SINS AS WHITE AS SNOW.
DOODLE A SKY FULL OF FLAKES! (CORN FLAKES?)

DOODLE WHAT YOU LIKE TO DO IN THE SNOW.
I GET YOUR DRIFT!

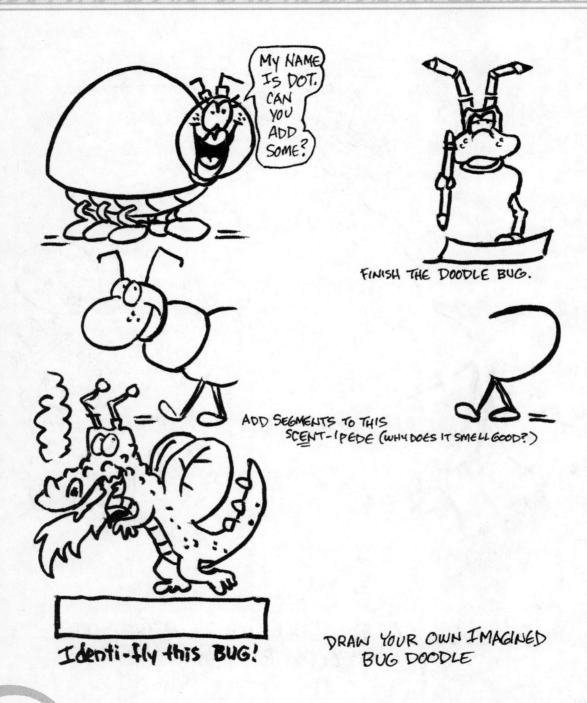

FINISH THE DOODLE BUG.

ADD SEGMENTS TO THIS SCENT-IPEDE (WHY DOES IT SMELL GOOD?)

Identi-fly this BUG!

DRAW YOUR OWN IMAGINED BUG DOODLE

THIS MIGHT BE THE VIEW IF A BUG STEPPED ON YOU. EWW. DOODLE A SHADOW OF YOU ON ITS BELLY.

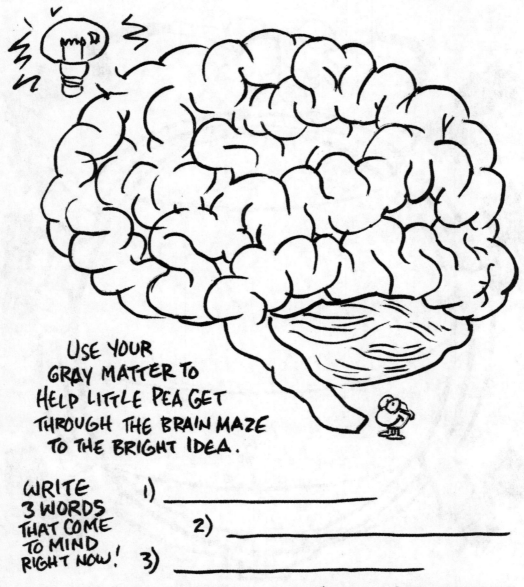

USE YOUR
GRAY MATTER TO
HELP LITTLE PEA GET
THROUGH THE BRAIN MAZE
TO THE BRIGHT IDEA.

WRITE
3 WORDS
THAT COME
TO MIND
RIGHT NOW!

1) _____

2) _____

3) _____

GOD HAD THE GREAT IDEA TO CREATE OUR BRAINS
AND PUT THEM IN OUR HEADS SO WE CAN MOVE AND THINK.

EVER HAD A BRAINSTORM? LIKE WHEN A GREAT
IDEA COMES TO MIND, IT'S SO EXCITING IT'S ELECTRIC!
WHEN THAT HAPPENS DRAW IT <u>HERE</u> & THANK **GOD!**

WHAT ELSE IS SPRINGING UP IN THE GARDEN?
DRAW THE VEGETATION ON THE SIGNS.

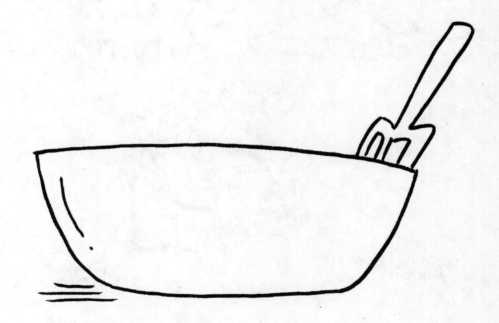

FILL THIS SALAD BOWL WITH
MIXED BLESSINGS... I MEAN - VEGETABLES!

FINISH THE BURNING BUSH! HOT!

DOODLE A PILLAR OF FIRE AT NIGHT!

AND MORE ISRAELITES!

GOD SPOKE TO MOSES FROM A BURNING BUSH,
HE LED HIS PEOPLE BY NIGHT WITH A FIERY PILLAR,
AND ONE DAY HE WILL JUDGE THE EARTH WITH FIRE.

ADD FLAMES TO THE LITTLE PICTURES TO SHOW HOW FIRE HAS BEEN USED, AND DOODLE EVEN MORE WAYS. YOU'RE GETTING WARMER!

GOD SHOWS HIS CAVERNOUS CREATIVITY IN CAVES.
WE SEE STALACTITES AND STALAGMITES AND STAY-BACK-
ITES (CRAWLERS WHO WON'T CRAWL ANY FURTHER).
LET'S EXPLORE YOUR CAVE DRAWINGS AND DOODLE-ITES.

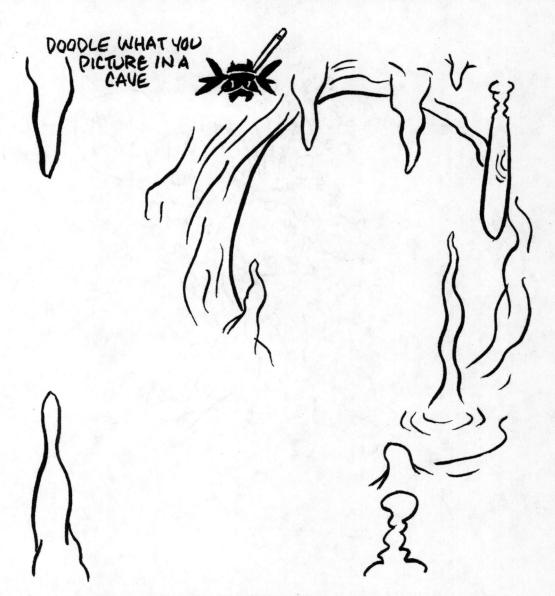

DOODLE WHAT YOU PICTURE IN A CAVE

OBADIAH WAS A "CAVE MAN"—HE HID 100 PROPHETS FROM JEZEBEL IN TWO CAVES. AND DAVID HID FROM SAUL IN A CAVE.

DOODLE MORE QUAKING MOUNTAINS WHO RUMBLE
WITH FEAR AND AWE BEFORE ALMIGHTY GOD.

DOODLE WHAT LIES IN THE MOUNTAIN RANGE.
HILLBILLY GOATS? FUR TREES? CAVES?

ADD SOME SUNSET WATCHERS ON SHORE. ADD SOME LINES IN THE SKY AND SOME COLOR... COTTON CANDY LIKE! MMM.

SUNSETS AND SUNRISES ARE BLESSINGS IN DA SKIES! THEY ARE COLORFUL SHOWCASES OF GOD'S BEAUTY AND MAJESTY. BREATHTAKING!

DOODLE A BEAUTIFUL SUNRISE

CAN WE GO TOUCH THE HORIZON, DAD?

COCK-A-DOODLE A ROOSTER COCK-A-DOODLE DOING!

SUNRISE IS A GREAT TIME TO TALK TO GOD... AND TO LISTEN.... AND SEE HIS AWESOME HANDIWORK! WHEN THE SUN RISES IT REMINDS US OF WHEN THE SON RISES.

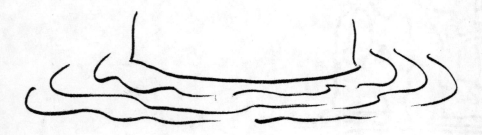

JOHN THE BAPTIST WORE A CAMEL'S HAIR COAT.
CAN YOU COVER FOR ME AND DOODLE IT?

CAN YOU DOODLE A BEAUTIFUL FUR
COAT FOR THE LADY? HOW 'BOUT A BEAVER COAT?

JESUS WANTS US TO BE "FISHERS OF MEN". TO DO THAT, WE HAVE TO USE OUR 'SWORDS' - THE BIBLE. DOODLE MORE FISH AND UNDERWATER LIFE. IT'S CATCHING!

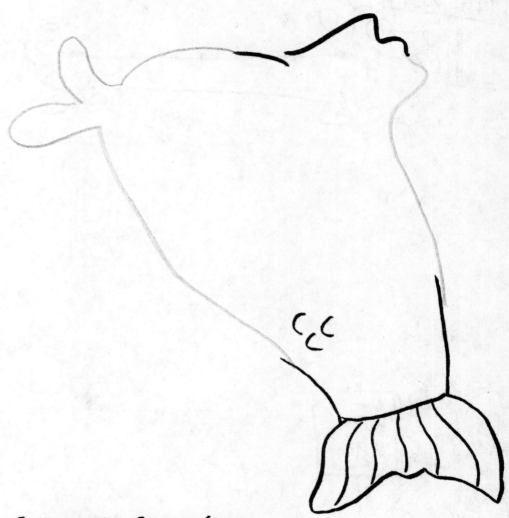

FINISH THIS GIANT FISH.
SPELL OUT ITS NAME WITH ITS SCALES.

DIFFERENT BREEDS OF DOGS DISPLAY GOD'S CREATIVITY. DOODLE DOGGIES... ALL THE MANY KINDS YOU CAN!! ARF!

BE A SAINT, BERNARD, AND DROOL ... I MEAN
DRAW BIG DOGS AND LITTLE ONES...YIP YIP YIP!

GOD SAYS FAITH THE SIZE OF A MUSTARD SEED CAN MOVE MOUNTAINS. SPELL OUT "FAITH" WITH MUSTARD SEEDS.

WHAT MOUNTAIN IN YOUR LIFE (HUGE OBSTACLE)
DO YOU NEED GOD TO MOVE TODAY? GOD
RELISHES IT WHEN WE'VE MUSTARD UP THE FAITH!
DOODLE THAT "MOUNTAIN" MOVING!

DRAW BONES IN THE EMPTY HOLES AND WRITE HIDDEN TALENTS ON THEM. DIG IT?

DOODLE YOURSELF DOING A TALENT
YOU THINK GOD HAS GIVEN YOU.

DOODLE LEAVES LEAVING THE TREE BECAUSE OF THE WIND.

WE DON'T KNOW WHICH WAY THE WIND BLOWS—BUT GOD DOES! JESUS CALMED THE WIND IN MARK 4:39, AND THE DISCIPLES WERE TERRIFIED THINKING, "WHO IS THIS THAT WIND AND WAVES OBEY HIM?!"

DOODLE A KITE IN THE SKY...
REALLY LET IT FLY ... CREATE SOME COOL DESIGNS.
DON'T FORGET THE TAIL. IS IT WAGGING?

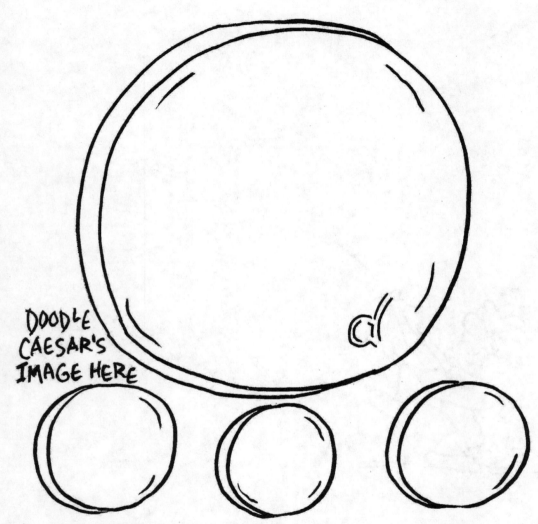

DOODLE CAESAR'S IMAGE HERE

MY SON, ZACH, LOVES TO CREATE COINS FROM CLAY AND THEN BAKES THEM IN THE OVEN. HE CREATIVELY ETCHES FRIENDS' IMAGES ON THEM. DO THAT HERE! IT MAKES CENTS!

DOODLE HIS FRIENDS RECEIVING COINS... PRICELESS!

WITH HIS COINS, ZACH CREATES CHRISTIAN FELLOWSHIP... THE GREEK WORD FOR IT IS... KOINONIA

1)

BIG HAIR, LITTLE HAIR, FLOCKS of FROCKS OR NO HAIR... GOD IS AWARE of EVERY HAIR THAT IS THERE!

2)　　　　　　　　3)

GET A HEAD START AND DOODLE THREE TYPES
OF HAIR. PONYTAILS? DREADLOCKS? FRIZZY?
STRAIGHT? FROSTED? HAIRY UP AND DRAW!

AARDVARK

WHAT IS HE THWACKING?

DUCK-BILLED PLATYPUS

DOODLE HIS BRO

WHAT'S IN PELICAN'S BEAK?

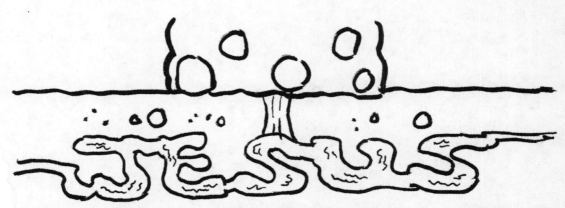

THE GREATEST UNDERGROUND TREASURE IS WATER...
AHHH!...WHICH EVERYONE NEEDS TO LIVE. FINISH THIS
WELL 'TIL IT'S WELL DONE AND DOODLE SPRINGS OF WATER
GUSHING UP. JESUS TELLS US HE IS THE LIVING WATER!

JOSHUA TREE

GOD GAVE US TREES FOR BEAUTY, OXYGEN, WIND BREAKS AND TO USE FOR OUR NEEDS — TO BUILD HOMES AND MAKE FURNITURE... AND EVEN BOOKS! YAY! DOODLE TREE-MENDOUS TREES!

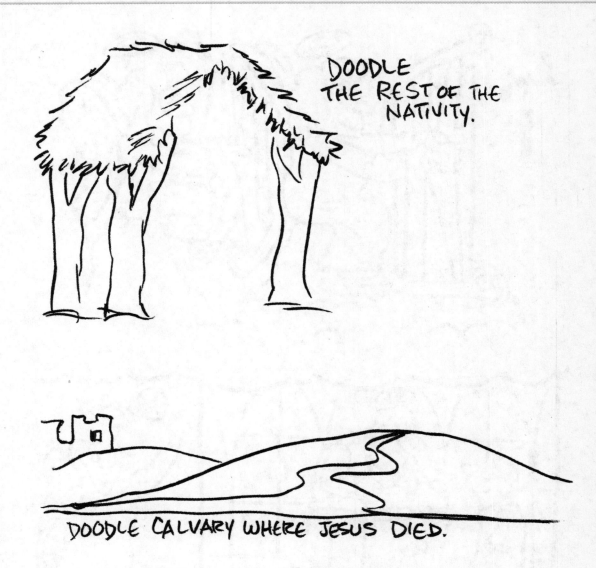

DOODLE THE REST OF THE NATIVITY.

DOODLE CALVARY WHERE JESUS DIED.

BUT, THE TWO GREATEST GIFTS FROM TREES WERE THESE:
- THE ONE THAT MADE A MANGER THAT HELD BABY JESUS
- THE ONE THAT BECAME A CROSS THAT LED TO OUR SALVATION.

HOW DO YOU PICTURE HEAVEN? IMAGINE AND DOODLE IT!

REVELATION 21 SAYS THE NEW JERUSALEM HAS PEARLY GATES AND STREETS OF GOLD. IN JOHN 14, JESUS SAYS, "MY FATHER'S HOUSE HAS MANY ROOMS...AND I'M GOING TO PREPARE A PLACE FOR YOU." IT WILL BE AWESOME!

Machu Picchu

MACHU PICCHU IS AN ANCIENT INCAN CITADEL
IN THE MOUNTAINS OF PERU. IT HAS BEEN NAMED
ONE OF THE NEW SEVEN WONDERS OF THE WORLD.

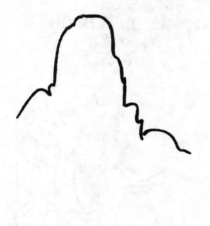

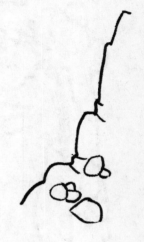

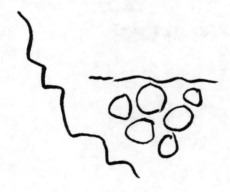

DOODLE A STONE CITY IN THE MOUNTAINS.
THIS LLAMA WILL HELP. BE A MACHU PICCHU
MAN — OR WOMAN!

GOD GAVE US ALL UNIQUE VOICES...
FROM THIS ONE'S BEAR-ITONE TO THIS ONE'S
MOUSEY
VOICE.

WHAT OTHER VOICES ARE THERE?

DOODLE A FROGGY VOICE   AND A HORSE ONE

WHAT IS YOUR VOICE LIKE? DOODLE IT! HOWEVER IT SOUNDS, LIFT IT UP IN PRAISE TO GOD. MAKE A CHOICE TO HONOR GOD WITH YOUR VOICE!

CREATE AN AWESOME TRAIL FOR
THESE RUNNERS. WHAT OBSTACLES CAN YOU MAKE?

WHEN WE RUN, WE GET GREAT EXCERCISE AND WE GET TO EXPERIENCE AND SEE GOD'S BEAUTIFUL HANDIWORK. NOW RUN ALONG AND BE IN AWE!! (NOT OWWW!)

Pig in a blanket

Pig in a Snuggie

DOODLE A CREATURE IN A COMFORTER (BLANKET)

WHAT IS HAPPENING? FINISH THE SCENE.

THE HOLY SPIRIT IS OUR COMFORTER. WHEN HE COMFORTS US, WE COMFORT OTHERS.

IN ARCHES NATIONAL PARK IN MOAB, UTAH, GOD MADE BEAUTIFUL SCULPTURES WITH SANDSTONE, WIND AND RAIN. DOODLE MORE NATURAL SCULPTURES. IT'S NOT HARD.

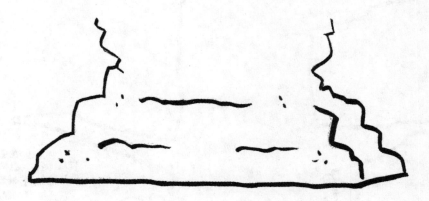

GOD GIVES US THE DREAM AND ABILITY TO SCULPT THINGS, TOO.
AND WHILE WE CHIP AWAY AT MARBLE, GOD CHIPS AWAY AT US-
SMOOTHING OUR ROUGH EDGES AND MAKING US MORE INTO THE
IMAGE OF CHRIST. (DON'T TAKE IT FOR GRANITE! ☺)
FINISH THIS EPIC SCULPTURE AND THE SCAFFOLD.

Family Tree

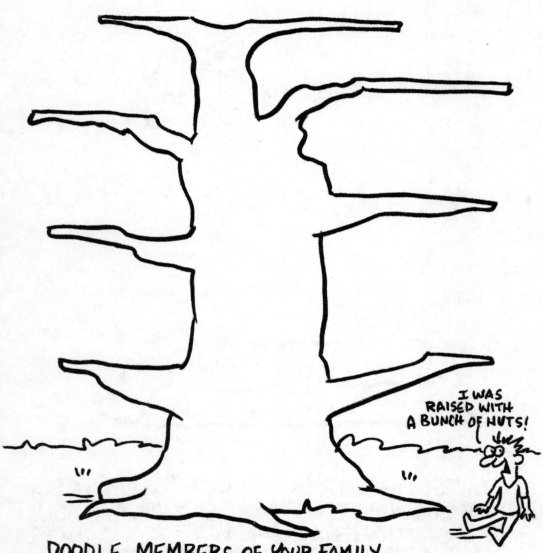

DRAW THE CROSS IN THE TREE.

I WAS RAISED WITH A BUNCH OF NUTS!

DOODLE MEMBERS OF YOUR FAMILY...
REALLY GO OUT ON A LIMB AND PUT THEM THERE!

DOODLE YOUR OWN SPOT-TO-SPOT PUZZLE.
HERE, I'LL SPOT YOU A FEW.

1)

2)

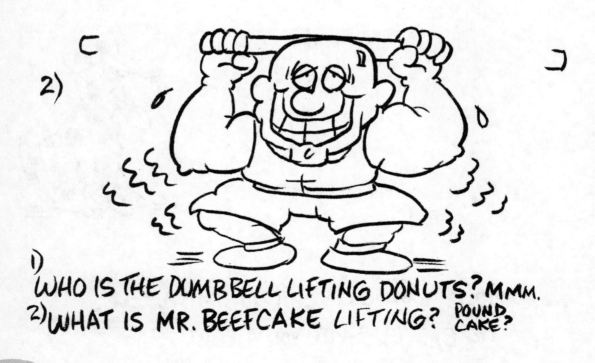

1) WHO IS THE DUMBBELL LIFTING DONUTS? MMM.
2) WHAT IS MR. BEEFCAKE LIFTING? POUND CAKE?

PEN SOMETHING POWERFUL THAT GOD
HAS CREATED!

LEONARDO DAVINCI
1452-1519

MAKE YOUR OWN
"MONA LISA"
OR BECKY OR RONELLE

DAVINCI WAS A PAINTER, SCIENTIST AND INVENTOR WHOSE IDEAS INSPIRED THE PARACHUTE, HELICOPTER AND MANY OTHER INVENTIONS.

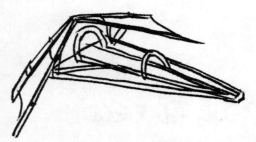

Design a Unique Flying machine

DISCOURAGED? PRESS ON!

IN THE BEGINNING...

1450
JOHANNES GUTENBERG

GUTENBERG, A GERMAN
BLACKSMITH, INVENTS MOVABLE
TYPE AND PUBLISHES THE BIBLE.

WRITE OUT
MORE OF THE BIBLE
IN FANCY TYPE.

A =   H =   O =   V =
B =   I =   P =   W =
C =   J =   Q =   X =
D =   K =   R =   Y =
E =   L =   S =   Z =
F =   M =   T =
G =   N =   U =

write something in your
new code language.

GOD GAVE PEOPLE GREAT MINDS SO THEY THEMSELVES
COULD BE GREAT CREATORS OR INVENTORS. INVENT YOUR OWN
ALPHABET.

WHEN WE WALK WITH THE LORD AND WE PLEASE HIM, WE BEAR GOOD FRUIT. DOODLE BEAR'S FRUIT. BEARIES?

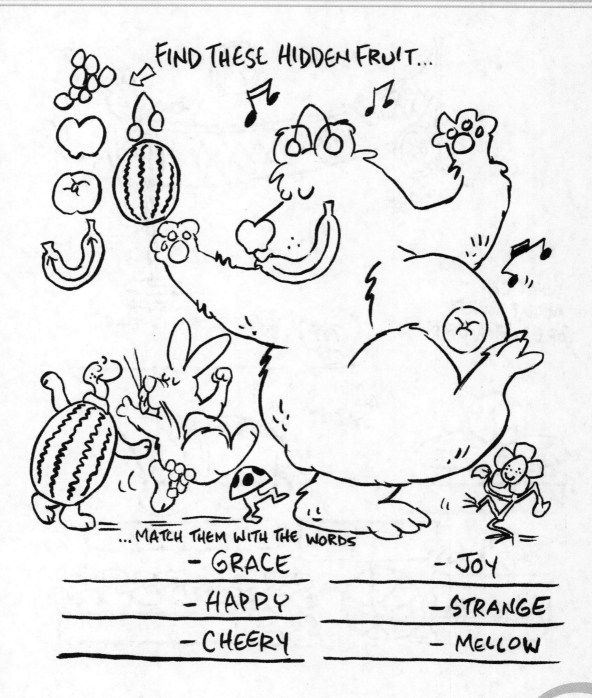

FIND THESE HIDDEN FRUIT...

...MATCH THEM WITH THE WORDS

- GRACE
- HAPPY
- CHEERY

- JOY
- STRANGE
- MELLOW

WHAT CAT IS ABOUT TO HIT (OR EAT) THE BIRDIE?

WHAT SPORT IS THIS?
← CLUE

NAME THAT SPORT

1.

2.

3.

4.

MAKE PICTURE PUZZLES FOR THESE SPORTS:

PING-PONG

CROQUET

JUMP ROPE

BOWLING

GOD HAS CREATED US TO COMPETE. HE HAS GIVEN MAN ABILITY TO CREATE SPORTS OF ALL SORTS. THIS VERSE SAYS WHEN WE COMPETE TO DO SO ACCORDING TO THE RULES. HEY SPORT, BE A GOOD SPORT AND COMPETE FOR CHRIST!

SPIDERS WEAVE WEB MASTERPIECES!
START AT THE CENTER AND FIND YOUR WAY TO THE
SAFETY SPOT. DON'T TOUCH LINES AND GET CAUGHT!

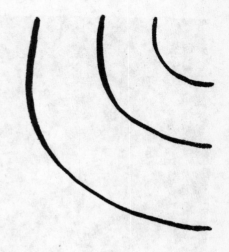

SEE IF YOU CAN HELP SPIDER SPIN AN AWESOME WEB. CAN YOU SPELL YOUR NAME IN IT? OTHERS? GOD HELPS US IF WE GET TRAPPED IN SATAN'S "WEBS," HIS SNARES AND LIES. HE IS THE LORD OF THE FLIES.

SOMETIMES IT MAY SEEM AS THOUGH BROTHERS AND SISTERS CAN REALLY GET IN THE WAY, BUT GOD CREATED THEM FOR A PURPOSE, TOO! DRAW YOU AND YOUR SIBLINGS.

GOD IS PLEASED WHEN WE HELP OUR
BROTHERS OR SISTERS. DOODLE YOU HELPING "YOUR
SISTER" IS A CAT HELPING, TOO? OR HACKING?

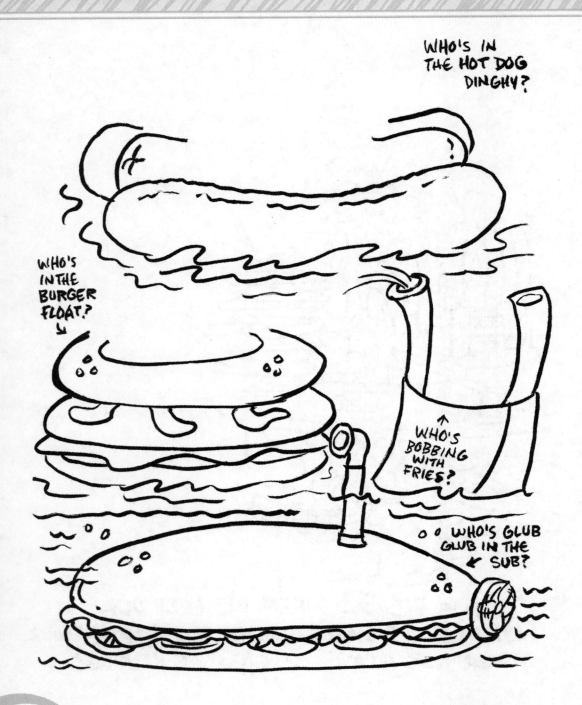

Add other
COOL AND YUMMY
POOL FLOATS

LET ME FLOAT
THIS PAST YOU.
SOMEONE HAS TO BE
HANGING OUT ON THE
BACON AND EGGS FLOATS.
BUT WHO? DOODLE IT.

GOD GAVE US ALL PERSONALITY TYPES - SHY, FRIENDLY, EXCITABLE, THOUGHTFUL, SILLY, MELLOW FELLOW... HOW DO YOU SEE YOURSELF?

ADD SOME PERSONALITY TO THESE CHARACTERS.
GOD WANTS US TO LOVE ALL KINDS... EVEN ON
THE SIDE!

DOODLE A COLORFUL NICKNAME YOU HAVE...
OR HAVE GIVEN, PUNKIN' HEAD!

JOHN SAYS THE VICTORIOUS BELIEVER WILL RECEIVE A NEW NAME IN HEAVEN. DOODLE NEW NAMES ON WHITE STONES. ROCKY? WRITE OUT YOUR NAME USING STONES.

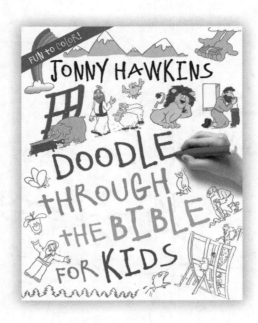

Oodles of Doodles to Do!

Have a bundle of fun and a laugh-out-loud good time while doodling your way through the Bible. With Jonny Hawkins' help and humor, you will explore God's Word in ways you've never done before. As you doodle your way through famous Bible stories, you will find it easier to remember important verses, sort out God's truth, and live God's way. With loads of humor and a big dose of fun, it's time to pick up a pencil, get creative, and *draw* closer to God!